One Hour Wordpower

Crisp, Clear Writing
in One Hour

ROBERT COOLE

Mandarin
in association with
The Sunday Times

A Mandarin Paperback
CRISP, CLEAR WRITING IN ONE HOUR

First published in Great Britain 1993
by Mandarin Paperbacks
an imprint of Reed Consumer Books Ltd
Michelin House, 81 Fulham Road, London SW3 6RB
and Auckland, Melbourne, Singapore and Toronto

Copyright © Graham King 1993
The right of Graham King to be identified
as the Author of these works has been asserted
in accordance with the Copyright, Designs
and Patents Act 1988

A CIP catalogue for this title
is available from the British Library

ISBN 0 7493 1521 0

Printed and bound in Great Britain
by Cox & Wyman Ltd, Reading, Berks

Contents

Acknowledgements

The author and publishers would like to thank the
following for their kind permission to reproduce
extracts:

Cassell plc: *The Second World War (VI): Triumph
and Tragedy*, by Sir Winston Churchill

Thames and Hudson Ltd: *A Good Enough Parent*,
by Bruno Bettelheim; copyright © 1987 Bruno
Bettelheim

Macmillan London Ltd: *The Way Through the
Woods*, by Colin Dexter; London 1992

Oxford University Press: *Fowler's Modern English
Usage* (Second Edition), ed. Sir Ernest Gowers;
Oxford 1965

The Plain English Campaign: *Gobbledegook – an
anthology of bureaucratic writing*, by Martin Cutts and
Chrissie Maher★

The *Daily Telegraph*: extracts pages 36–7, 42, 43–4
copyright © The Telegraph plc 1992

The *Sunday Telegraph*: extract pages 81–2 copyright
© The Telegraph plc 1992

The *Independent*: extracts pages 36, 44, 82–3
copyright © The Independent 1992

The *Sun*: extract page 81 copyright © The Sun 1992

The publishers have made every endeavour to trace
the owners of copyright and apologise for any
inadvertent omissions.

★The Plain English Campaign was founded by Mrs
Chrissie Maher, who had been illiterate until she
was sixteen. It wages non-stop war on obscure and
confusing language in official and other public
writings. Address: Outram House, Canal Street,
Whaley Bridge, Stockport SK12 7LS.

Introduction
Into the jungle, with machete and cleft stick

Let us be brave. We are about to hack our way into a
jungle. The dense, tangled world of obscure and
difficult language. Officialese. Jargon. Circumlocution.
Verbiage. Pomposity. Cliché. All the ugly growths that
prevent us understanding a piece of writing.

Perhaps the obstacle is a letter from the town council,
which for all we know might have a drastic effect on
our future.

Perhaps a newspaper story which makes us stop and
re-read, seeking its meaning.

Or perhaps an advertisement for a job we might fancy
. . . if only we knew what the wording meant.

This guide, though, is not meant to help the baffled
reader to fight his way through the thickets of spiky
legalisms, prickly abstractions and choking verbosity.

It is an effort to help you, the **writer** of the letter,
memo, report, manifesto, survey or press release, to
make sure your writing is cleared of such obstacles to
understanding.

Don't be a sloppy copycat

In business and bureaucracies, it is easy to fall in with
the writing habits of everyone else around you: sloppy,
vague and clumsy.

A letter, memo or report from someone who is known
to write clearly and with precision will obviously be
more welcome, and read more keenly, than a dreary
wodge of waffle and obscurity.

Your own writing will be most effective when it is clear
and direct. People who write in a straightforward way
always shine out against the dim grey mass of Sloppies.

As a writer, you have to be tighter

The usual advice on clear expression is: 'Write as you

speak.' That advice is sound enough – but in everyday conversation we do not generally need the clarity and precision we should aim for in the written word, which cannot be helped along with the odd smile, shrug, frown or particular tone of voice.

Perhaps the advice should be amended slightly, to: 'Write as you speak – but make it tighter.'

People can lose sight of the purpose of putting something in writing. The purpose is usually not to compose a fancy array of words, but to say what you mean. Clarity can be its own form of elegance.

Before you begin to write, THINK –

- What do I want to say?
- Am I making just one main point, or several?
- If several, what's the order of importance?

You may find it worthwhile to jot down your points before starting your letter, notice, press release or story. If you use a word processor, of course, it may be just as easy to get all your thoughts down first, then sort them into an acceptable order, on the screen. (*See* Wonders of the Word Processor, p. 95.)

It is easy to confuse even the simplest message by using language that is not clear, or to lose the reader's attention by being too complicated – or simply going on too long.

Sometimes, of course, it may be undesirable to be too clear and concise, if your words are likely to commit you or your employers to something better avoided. Even then, you should be clear exactly what you are trying not to say, and why. That kind of imprecision requires skill, not mere sloppiness.

The shorter the better, but don't be a machine-gun

Your English will be clearer and crisper if, in the main, you keep your sentences short. But this can be overdone. Short sentences, yes. But not all the time. Otherwise your reader may feel he or she is being sprayed with a machine-gun.

A 'crescendo' effect of short and longer sentences – for example, short/short/shortish/long – makes easier, more interesting reading:

> The vicar looked strained. The usual smile was missing. Mrs Parrot had no idea what might be the matter. But she was determined to get to the bottom of it, before going home that night.

Take a tip from a master-novelist

But they didn't devote the whole evening to music. After a while, they played at forfeits; for it is good to be children sometimes, and never better than at Christmas, when its mighty Founder was a child himself. Stop! There was first a game at blind-man's buff. Of course there was. And I no more believe Topper was really blind than I believe he had eyes in his boots.

Charles Dickens, *A Christmas Carol*

The English language can be a bewildering jungle, if you let it. But there are plenty of markers to guide us. If we keep our nerve steady, our eyes wide open and our cutting-blade sharp, together we can hack a way through . . . and emerge into the sunny glade of clear, concise English.

And, once safely back to the relative civilisation of the office, with the machete and cleft stick stowed in the stationery cupboard, how satisfying to stand at the copier with your crisp, fresh document . . . watching as a less well-schooled colleague's handiwork, sodden with cliché, drenched in jargon, swamped with officialese, comes oozing out of that machine.

From Here to Obscurity: The Baffling Art of Officialese

If language can be a jungle, officialese is the minefield laid among the thorny thickets and clinging creepers of that jungle. Faced with a mass of pure officialese, the bravest of us is likely to radio for a rescue helicopter.

Despite the successes of the Plain English Campaign, officials in government, local councils and other bureaucratic organisations still too often try to lure us into their own well-loved, baffling word mazes.

A railway announcer may proclaim: *Due to an earlier person on the line, trains will be subject to intervals.*

Intervals between services are certainly a sound way of avoiding collisions: otherwise the announcement is typical, thoughtless officialese.

The language of officialdom can obliterate all meaning. Feel the undergrowth closing in, as you try to fight your way out of this tiger trap dug by the Department of Health and Social Services . . .

Case of the crippled sentence

> A person shall be treated as suffering from physical disablement such that he is either unable to walk or virtually unable to do so if he is not unable or virtually unable to walk with a prosthesis or an artificial aid which he habitually wears or uses or if he would not be unable or virtually unable to walk if he habitually wore or used a prosthesis or an artificial aid which is suitable in his case.

> taken from *Gobbledygook*,
> published by the Plain English Campaign

This would-be 'sentence' first of all reflects a legalistic terror of punctuation: the full stop or comma which,

10

misplaced, might lead the Department all the way to a House of Lords appeal.

Let us take our machete to the undergrowth, bring in the wire-cutters, and try to discover what, if anything, this passage struggles to convey. A step at a time, for fear of booby-traps.

A person shall be treated as suffering from physical disablement . . . treated? This is not intended as medical advice, but since the background is medical, the reader may, however briefly, be confused. Lift out *treated*. Replace it with *considered*. And that chance of confusion disappears.

Suffering from physical disablement Why not simply *physically disabled*? And while we are at it, we don't need *as* after *considered*. Pluck it out, hurl it into the jungle shrubbery.

So far, in our cleaned-up version, we have 'A person shall be considered physically disabled' – and we don't seem to have lost any of the intended meaning.

Such that he is either unable to walk or virtually unable to do so Wrench away the clumsy *such that he is* and replace it with *which makes him*. Next, we cut out *either* – because we don't need it.

We now have 'which makes him unable to walk, or virtually unable to do so.' More tightly expressed as 'which makes him unable, or virtually unable, to walk'.

Peering into the gloom, we next tackle *if he is not unable or virtually unable to walk with a prosthesis or an artificial aid which he habitually wears or uses . . .* Stop! The rest is just the gibbering of jungle monkeys. This seems to mean that the poor chap can get around, but only with the help of a prosthesis or other artificial aid. The word *even*, before *if he is not* would have helped. But we simply do not need this tangled heap of words at all.

The entire 'sentence', if it means anything, must surely mean this:

> A person is regarded as physically disabled if he
> always needs an artificial aid to walk.

This was a prime example of the need to think 'What
do I want to say?' And then to say it, the simple way.

A serious case of effluxion

From a London borough council, this smokescreen:

> And take further notice that under the provisions
> of Section 47(2) of the said Housing Act 1974 in
> relation to any land consisting of or including Hous-
> ing Accommodation in a Housing Action Area, a
> landlord must not less than four weeks before the
> expiry by effluxion of time of any tenancy which
> expires without the service of any Notice to Quit,
> notify the council in writing that the tenancy is
> about to expire in accordance with the said schedule
> 4 · · ·

A model of mixed officialese and legalese: you can
almost see the glint of watch-and-chain on the Town
Clerk's egg-stained black waistcoat. How do we turn it
into something like English, without losing any legal
force the passage might be required to have?

For a start, there seems no need for *And take further
notice*. If the reader is not going to take notice, there
seems little point in the writer finishing his masterwork.
Next: *under the provisions of Section 47(2) of the said
Housing Act 1974* – the words *the provisions of* are
redundant. Let's lose them. The same goes for *said*.

And next: *in relation to any land consisting of or
including*. The lawyers can keep their *consisting of or
including*, just in case they are struggling to cover, say,
a backyard where someone lives in a caravan. But *in
relation to* can shorten to *concerning*.

We have now brought *concerning* clumsily close to

consisting, so let us replace *consisting of* with *that consists of*. The word *Accommodation* after *Housing* is not needed. And once *Housing* is left standing by itself, the capital H becomes even more obviously unnecessary.

Plodding on: *a landlord must not less than four weeks before the expiry by effluxion of time* . . . Quickly to the dictionary, to seek out this excitingly unfamiliar word, *effluxion*. We find:

> Efflux, n. Flowing out (of liquid, air, gas: also fig.)
> That which flows out. Hence effluxion, n).

From its meaning the word suits the prose style, if nothing else. But we can do without *effluxion*. We can also do without *expiry*.

Now, what is the rest of the council's message?

It seems to be that in a Housing Action Area, if a landlord knows that a tenancy is running out, and no notice to quit is needed, he must warn the council in writing, at least four weeks before that tenancy is due to end.

Let us tack that piece of information on to our earlier repair:

> Under Section 47(2) of the Housing Act 1974, concerning any land that consists of or includes housing in a Housing Action Area, if a landlord knows that a tenancy is due to end without need of a notice to quit, he must tell the council in writing at least four weeks before the tenancy runs out.

Still scarcely slick or smooth. But perhaps a shade less forbidding than the original mess.

How axiomatic is your bus shelter?

From the West Yorkshire Passenger Transport Executive:

I refer to your recent letter in which you submit a request for the provision of a bus passenger shelter in Ligett Lane at the inward stopping place for Service 31 adjacent to Gledhow Primary School. The stated requirement for a shelter at this location has been noted, but as you may be aware shelter erection at all locations within West Yorkshire has been constrained in recent times as a result of instructions issued by the West Yorkshire Metropolitan County Council in the light of the Government's cuts in public expenditure and, although it seems likely that the Capital Budget for shelter provision will be enhanced in the forthcoming Financial Year, it is axiomatic that residual requests in respect of prospective shelter sites identified as having priority, notably those named in earlier programmes of shelter erection will take precedence in any future shelter programme.

Let us briefly mop our brows and try to fathom what the poor, befuddled author was battling to say, before we set about helping him say it in English.

At a guess, the passage could be summed up as:

I refer to your request for a bus shelter in Ligett Lane . . . Unfortunately, because of Government spending cuts, West Yorkshire Metropolitan County Council has in turn ordered a curb on bus-shelter building. Although there may be more money for such work in our next financial year, shelters already on the waiting list will obviously be built first.

Where did the author go wrong? Let us lay this Frankenstein's Monster on the slab, and dissect:

I refer to your recent letter in which you submit a request for the provision of a bus passenger shelter in Ligett Lane . . . If the writer identifies the subject clearly enough, there is no need to remind his correspondent of all the details. The correspondent wants a Yes, No or even Maybe – with an explanation, if the answer is No or Maybe.

The stated requirement for a shelter at this location has been noted. Of course it has. Otherwise, the official would hardly be writing at all.

but as you may be aware . . . Word-wasting. It doesn't matter if the correspondent is *aware* or not. Your job is to make sure he knows the facts now.

shelter erection at all locations within West Yorkshire has been constrained in recent times . . . No purpose is served by *at all locations*. There is no reason to use *within* rather than *in*, no matter how widely this particular verbal fungus has spread.

constrained should be replaced by the easier-to-take *restricted*.

in recent times is another redundancy. So is *as a result of instructions issued by*.

Granted that *West Yorkshire Metropolitan County Council* is rendered with a rare and forceful clarity, not a syllable wasted. But then we slide back into the Monster's pit . . . *in the light of the Government's cuts in public expenditure* . . . The only meaning of *in the light of*, here, is *because of*. Your reader, rightly or not, will still blame the Government for the lack of a bus shelter, whether you use the clear or the foggy expression. So why go for the fog? (See *Fog Index*, p. 86)

and, although it seems likely that the Capital Budget for shelter provision will be enhanced in the forthcoming Financial Year . . . The reader is less interested in what the bus-shelter fund is called, than what it will do for him, and when. Ditch *the Capital Budget*. And since a shelter is a shelter, *provision* is yet another unneeded word.

enhanced, in this context, means *increased*. There seems no reason to evade the more common word.

it is axiomatic that An axiom is a self-evident truth. *Axiomatic* is presumably meant to convey *self-evidently true.* If something is that obvious, the writer is wasting his Transport Executive's paper and his reader's time in saying it.

residual requests in respect of prospective shelter sites identified as having priority, notably those named in earlier programmes of shelter erection Hurling a swift grenade into the middle of this, we are left with *Shelter requests not met by earlier building programmes.*

will take precedence in any future shelter programme. Not much, for once, to argue with there – apart, perhaps, from the repetition of *shelter programme.*

The deskbound, wordbound Frankenstein who created our Monster may be sad, even annoyed, at the way we have slimmed down his offspring. But at least he can now discover what he really meant to say.

Q and A to save the day

None of the sorry examples quoted need have happened, if only the writers had held this conversation with themselves:

Q What's it all about?

A It's about when somebody is classed as disabled/ special duty of a landlord in a Housing Action Area/ someone wanting a bus shelter built.

Q What do we want to say?

A We want to say that someone who can't walk unaided is officially disabled/ Housing Action Area landlord has to warn the council when there's about to be a tenancy available/ we can't afford the requested bus shelter just now.

Q Very well. Why don't we just SAY it!

Jargon: smart talk that soon gets tiresome

Jargon – words and phrases which may have started life among a particular circle of people, trade or profession, but spread among others who wish to appear up-to-date.

The Concise Oxford Dictionary explains jargon as 'unintelligible words, gibberish; barbarous or debased language; mode of speech full of unfamiliar terms; twittering of birds.'

Not all jargon is that dreadful, and there is no harm in using a little, every so often. But a lot of it is just a distortion of language – and that can only interfere with meaning.

Some of the worst modern jargon is spoken, rather than written. It is hard to imagine even the most modish jargonaut writing down disc-jockey nonsense such as: 'The time at this hour is twenty-five ahead of the witching hour of twelve noon.'

Technical terms, used among experts as a shorthand language, are not jargon of the kind we are discussing – however opaque they may seem to outsiders. But there are less excusable vogue expressions that have encrusted the language, and we should all take the chisel to them.

Help wanted in the job-ads swamp

Company advertisements offering jobs have created their own hideous swamp of non-language.

cultivational – a fortunately rare sighting, in an English National Opera advertisement for a 'development officer – events', to be responsible for *co-ordinating and administering cultivational and fundraising events*. It is just possible that *cultivational* really means something. Our only guess is that it is something to do with sucking up to people to get them to put some money into a project. Your guess, obviously, is just as good.

driven – as in *quality-driven service organisation*. As with *orientated* (see below), this is merely meant to indicate the firm's sense of priority – in this case, to produce high-quality goods or services.

environment, meaning, usually, the place where the worker will do the job. The firm which boasted a *quality-driven organisation* also promised . . . *a demanding and results orientated environment*. Another company required a background of *progressive sales or marketing environment*. In this case, *environment* presumably meant *business*. In which case, *sales or marketing* would have sufficed. *Progressive* can only mean forward-looking – and few firms are to be found in need of backward-looking candidates.

Should have experience in a fast-moving, multi-assembly environment. Assuming that *multi-assembly* has its own recognisable meaning in the business concerned, why not simply require *experience in fast multi-assembly?*

Environmental hazard on the line

London Underground Ltd, advertising for a Director of Human Resources (see below), demanded *broadly based blue-chip HR experience in unionised environment*. Apart from the *blue chip* nonsense, presumably meaning senior level in a successful company, London Underground clearly wanted someone experienced at dealing with trade unions. In which case, why not say so?

Human Resources (people). Replacement for *personnel*, which, though also bureauspeak, at least does not have the ghastly pretentiousness and pseudo-caringness of *Human Resources*.

motivated is one of the most hard-worked jargon words in job advertisements . . . *the ability to motivate, lead and be an effective team player; management and motivation of the sales force; should be self-motivated.* In the first two examples, we can substitute *inspire* and *inspiration*. In the third, it is harder to guess what the applicant will be required to prove. *Enterprising*, perhaps. Or *should show initiative*. Or, if those sound too revolutionary for the company's taste, *able to work unsupervised*.

pivotal role. Fancier version of *key role*. Neither means much, to explain a job. If the importance of the post needs to be stressed, what's wrong with *important*?

positive discrimination (favour/preference)

orientated, as in *results-orientated environment* (see *environment*, above). The word is presumably meant to convey what the firm considers important. In this example, its use is *nonsense-orientated*. A company that is not keen on getting results will not be placing job advertisements for much longer. So the whole phrase can be cut out.

Another advertisement required someone *success-orientated*. There is a perfectly good word to replace that: *ambitious*.

postholder (employee)

proactive, mostly found in social services advertisements, describing the approach to a particular job. It means initiating change where needed, as opposed to merely responding to events – *reactive*. Difficult to think of a crisp equivalent, but at least we can try to keep the word out of our everyday language.

remit, meaning *responsibility*. It may be shorter, but is not otherwise commonly used, and is pompous.

remuneration package simply means *salary and perks*. If *perks* is too racy, try *other benefits*. Lots of companies do!

skills At first sight, a reasonable word to expect in job advertisements. There are, though, some odd uses, as in *interpersonal skills*, which presumably means *good at dealing with people*.

specific, as in *The main duties of the post will include: developing country-specific and/or product-specific marketing activity plans*. That, heaven help us, came from an advertisement by the personnel department of the University of Cambridge Local Examinations syndicate. They could have said: *Developing plans for selling to particular countries and/or selling particular batches of information*.

structured, as in *it is likely that you will have worked successfully in a sizeable, structured organisation*. You would hardly go recruiting in an *un*-structured organisation.

Of all jargon, among the most impenetrable can be found in council social services departments. An advertisement about a home for teenagers: *The aim of the home is to enable older young people who still have substantial emotional and personal deficits to make planned progress towards personal autonomy* . . .

Even from social worker to social worker, this is garbled nonsense. Surely no professional catastrophe will happen if we simply say: *to enable teenagers with troubled personalities to learn to cope for themselves*.

A splatter of multiculturals

experience of managing a multicultural urban
environment and the ability to integrate equalities
considerations into areas of work activity.

This passage, from an advertisement for a Deputy
Director of Social Services, is a real polysyllabic mess.
Multicultural urban environment, despite modern
delicacies, simply means *racially-mixed part of town*. And
integrate may mean here *build in*. Or it may have been
misused to mean *include*.

Every trade is entitled to its own jargon . . . up to a
point. So let us allow that *equalities* is immediately
understood among social services people as meaning
equal treatment regardless of race, sex and, probably,
physical handicaps – though *equality* in the singular
serves the purpose as well, or better.

That passage, converted into plain English, could
read:

Experience of dealing with a racially-mixed town
area and ability to ensure that equality is part of
departmental life.

The same advertisement required *ability to organise
intervention in the community to establish the needs of
potential service users*. Meaning, presumably, *ability to
go out and find what people need us to do*.

Social workers do not have the battlefield to themselves,
when it comes to jargon. An advertisement for a health
worker in Brazil said:

You will assist the team in formulating and
implementing a health policy, evaluating and
developing appropriate responses to specific health
problems in indigenous areas . . .

Meaning: *You will help to plan and carry out a policy to deal with health problems among local people.*

A breathless advertisement by the English National Board for Nursing, Midwifery and Health Visiting, seeking a director of midwifery education, brought the equivalent of motorway carnage to the English language:

> essential qualities include innovative abilities, proven inter-personal and communication skills, an energetic pursuance of goals and a positive approach.

What a spectacular pile-up! What on earth *were* they looking for?

Computerspeak horrors

From the world of computers, source of some of the worst non-language, comes:

> Driven and focused by seeing the world from the customer's perspective, we continue to build an organisation where quality is embedded in every aspect of endeavour . . .

From the same advertisement:

> Our continued growth in the network computing industry mandates that we now identify and attract the most talented and creative Sales and Marketing Professionals . . .

Mandates? This announcement sounds as if it was written by someone for whom English was not the first language, and whose dictionary had a bad coffee-stain on the relevant entry.

Perhaps those who draft such monstrosities should

study this one, tucked among the large, expensive advertisements in the same newspaper's pages:

> KITCHEN DESIGNER (Trainee considered) for thriving Chelsea Studio. Drawing experience essential. Salary negotiable dependent on experience. If you are aged 20–30, educated to at least A-level standard, have a bright personality, thrive on hard work and are happy to work Saturdays, tell me about yourself by leaving a message on my Ansaphone, not forgetting to leave your phone no., or write with brief CV to . . .

Bright. Un-pompous. Direct. And above all, *clear*.

Jargonaut's lexicon

The nastiest entries are graded with **j** symbols – more **j**s, worse jargon.

accessible, as in *make Shakespeare accessible to the millions* (understandable/attractive) [j]

activist, as in *political party activist* (worker/campaigner)

address, as in *address the problem* (tackle, face, deal with) [j]

airlifted (flown). *Airlift* was originally military jargon for a bulk movement of materials or people by plane. It is hardly warranted in describing, say, a helicopter flight taking a road casualty to hospital. [j]

ahead of, as in *shares rose ahead of the company report* (rose before the company report was published/over expectations from the company report) [j]

albeit (even if/although)

all that jazz (and so on/etcetera) [j]

at risk, as in *these children are on the at-risk register* (danger)

blueprint, as in *this is a blueprint for disaster* (this will end in/means/could mean disaster)

bullish (confident) [j]

cash-strapped/strapped for cash (hard up/short of money) [j]

chair/chairperson (chairman/chairwoman) [jj]

chauvinism – originally obsessive patriotism, after Napoleon-worshipper Nicolas Chauvin. Nowadays usually refers to *male chauvinism*, a vogue expression meaning a man's unwarranted belief in his automatic superiority over women (male arrogance) [j]

come on stream, as in *the new model Rolls Royce will come on stream in April*. Suitable enough as oil-producer's jargon, but now often misapplied to some unlikely fields, from bus production to new radio stations and hospitals (begin production/start working/get under way/open for business) [j]

come to terms with (accept/understand)

concept (idea/notion/plan/proposal) [j]

core curriculum (basic curriculum) [j]

cutback – needless expansion of cut [j]

de-manning (cutting jobs) [jjj]

de-stocking (letting stocks dwindle/shrink/run down) [jjj]

down that road, as in *if we go down that road, what will happen?* (if we do that) [j]

downplay, as in *he tried to downplay the gravity of the case* (play down/minimise/belittle) [jj]

end of the day, as in *at the end of the day, what have we got?* (in the end – or just cut it out!) [j]

24

final analysis, as with *in the final analysis, it makes no difference* (treat as for *end of the day*) [j]

funded (paid for, backed, supported) [j]

geared to (suited to) [j]

go for the burn (go all out/make the last big effort) [jjj]

go through channels (get authority/follow correct routine) [j]

hands-on, as in *he adopted a hands-on approach to his job as manager*. This seems to mean no more than *he did the job he was paid to do, rather than sit back in his office with the cocktail cabinet permanently open*. A less respectful meaning, possibly in the minds of staff working for this hands-on hero, might be *He's always on our backs and under our feet*. There seems no real need for this expression. [jj]

heading up – use *heading* or *leading*. The *up* is mere cottonwool. [j]

innovative – applied to a person, this presumably means someone with bright ideas – a little longer, certainly, but more immediately understood. Applied to a product, project or work of art or literature, there seems little wrong with *novel*, *inventive* or even *new*, according to context. [jj]

An acute case of the inputs

A core post is available for a Senior Research Associate to take a leading role in the programme. The first projects involve relating nursing inputs to patient outcomes in acute hospitals.

University of Newcastle upon Tyne advertisement

---

input – horrid germ picked up from the computer world, where it is used as a verb meaning *enter*, as in *he inputted the whole file into the computer*. Now likely to turn up elsewhere, as in *planned input of personal supervision*. At best the word means *contribution*. At worst, as in this example, it means nothing. [jjjj]

insightful (perceptive/shrewd) [j]

interface. As a noun, just means *contact*. As a hideous verb, *interface with* means *negotiate with*, *discuss with* or *meet*. Any of these is preferable. [jjjj]

jury is still out, as in *as to whether this move has saved Sterling, the jury is still out* (is not yet known/decided/certain/clear) [j]

logistics, as in the *logistics of the situation* (practicalities) [j]

meet with/meet up with (meet) [j]

methodology (absurd way to convey method) [j]

name of the game, as in *the name of the game is making money* (object) [jj]

new high (new/record high level/height) [j]

new low (new/record low level/depth) [j]

non-stopping, as in *eastbound services will be non-stopping at the following stations* . . . (will not stop) [jjj]

operational, as in *eastbound services are now fully operational* (now working/running) [j]

outgoing (friendly) [j]

overview (broad view) [j]

no way, as in *no way will I do that* – irritating, dated way to say *I will not* [j]

on the back of, as in *shares rose sharply on the back of a good profit forecast* (after/because of) [jj] *ongoing*, as in *we have an ongoing supply problem* (continuing) [j]

pre-condition – a condition is something that has to happen before something else will happen. It is not possible to impose a condition on the past. So *pre-condition*, however popular among politicians (*there must be no pre-conditions for the peace talks*) is nonsense (condition) [jjj]

proven – so rarely used in real language that there seems no excuse for preferring it to *proved*. Certainly it should never have appeared in, of all contexts, a BBC advertisement for a sub-editor with *proven journalistic skills*. Let us hope they found one whose *proven skills* enable him or her to spot irritating jargon at a thousand paces. [j]

put in place (ready/get ready/prepare) [j]

put on the back burner (put off/put back) [jj]

set to, as in *The Emperor was reported to be set to abdicate* (expected to, intending to, about to)

spend, as in *a total advertising spend*. An abbreviation no doubt meant to convey the need for terribly-important executives to save syllable time (expenditure, spending) [jj]

state of the art (newest/latest) [jj]

take on board (accept/understand/comprehend) [j]

terminal (fatal) [j]

track record – except for an athlete, perhaps, *track* record means nothing more than *record*. The next time you draft such an advertisement, be a pioneer: shun *proven track record*. *Experience* will normally do. [j]

user-friendly (easy to use) [j]

viable alternative (alternative/choice/option) [jj]

within, as in *a minimum of 5 years marketing experience within a quality-driven service organisation* (in) (see also *driven*, above) [j]

So long, scenario

Scenario has lately been distorted from its real meaning, which is an outline of a play or film.

- *worst-case scenario* (at worst)
- *completely different scenario* (different sequence of events)
- *scenario for World War Three* (How World War Three might happen)

Depending on context, you can use *prediction*, *programme* or *plan*.

Reach for the de-iser

One increasingly popular and lazy habit is the addition of *ise* to create a verb. Sometimes this does not get in the way of meaning, but at other times it does.

Some *ise* words are part of our orthodox language – for example, *idolise*, *mechanise*, *mobilise*. But in recent years the *ise* has been tacked on, less comfortably, to other words.

normalise, though not much used by real people, is probably too much part of the language of politicians to be got rid of. The humbler of us can make do with *return/get back to normal*.

hospitalise is still rarely heard in Britain, and long may that be so. For conveying direct meaning to the reader, it can never replace *taken to hospital*.

unionise is probably in the same class as *normalise*.

criminalise (transform non-criminal behaviour into criminal), like *politicise* (draw a person or topic into

28

politics), fortunately seems to remain the verbal property of political agitators and social workers who presumably understand each other.

marginalise, meaning *belittle* or *push to one side*.

None of these invented noun-plus-ise 'words' helps clarity.

When in is out
in-flight/in-house/in-car

As with *in-flight movie*, where, assuming we are talking to air passengers, only *movie* or *film* is needed.

As with *brochures produced in-house* – meaning *by the company's own staff* or *on the company's premises*. Using the jargon, we may save a few words. Without it, the meaning will be more immediately obvious to people who do not use it themselves.

As with *in-car entertainment*, grandiose way of saying a radio and tape cassette/CD player. Even retaining entertainment, we can at least get rid of that intrusive *in-*.

In-car has not yet invaded the language as thoroughly as *in-flight* or *in-house*. But these expressions, too, were once as unfamiliar as they are ugly. It would be a bold gambler who bet against *in-car* becoming part of our common speech.

Circumlocution – The Long, Long Trail A-winding

> Bournemouth was on Monday night thrown into a state of most unusual gloom and sorrow by the sad news that the Rev. A.M. Bennett – who for the last 34 years has had charge of St Peter's Church and parish, and who has exercised so wonderful an influence in the district – had breathed his last, and that the voice which only about a week previously had been listened to by a huge congregation at St Peter's was now hushed in the stillness of death . . .
>
> *Lymington Chronicle*, January 22, 1880

When a writer or speaker fills you with the urge to shout 'Get on with it!', he or she is probably committing the sin of circumlocution. Even in the most purple of today's newspapers, the example above would be a collector's item.

Politicians, of course, are notable circumlocutionists: they often have a keen interest in not being pinned down. Not so long ago, a British political leader went on television to explain his attitude to the introduction of a single currency for all countries in the European Community.

Before you continue reading, it might be as well to find a comfortable seat . . .

> 'No, I would not be signing up: I would have been making, and would be making now, a very strong case for real economic convergence, not the very limited version which the Conservatives are offering, so we understand, of convergence mainly of inflation rates, important though that is, but of convergence across a range of indicators – base rates, deficits and, of course, unemployment – together

with a number of indexes of what the real performance of economies are . . .'

(Perhaps a brief tea-break would be in order here.)

'. . . the reason I do that and the reason why that
is an argument that must be won before there is any
significant achievement of union is not only a British
reason, although it is very important to us, it is a
European Community reason: if we were to move
towards an accomplished form of union over a very
rapid timetable without this convergence taking
place it would result in a two-speed Europe, even
to a greater extent than now – fast and slow, rich
and poor – and the fragmentation of the Community, which is the very opposite of what those
people who most articulate the view in favour of
integration and union really want; when I put that
argument to my colleagues in, for instance, the Fed-
eration of Socialist Parties, many of whom form the
governments in the EC, there is a real understanding and agreement with that point of view . . .'

So what precisely might the gentleman have been
hoping to convey? Probably this:

'I do not want a single European currency until
various other factors affecting the question have
been dealt with. The factors are these . . .'

America's then President, George Bush, was of course
famous for his bemusing circumlocution, as in this
speech defending his accomplishments:

'I see no media mention of it, but we entered in –
you asked what time it is and I'm telling you how
to build a watch here – but we had Boris Yeltsin
in here the other day, and I think of my times
campaigning in Iowa, years ago, and how there was

31

a – I single out Iowa, it's kind of an international state in a sense and has a great interest in all these things – and we had Yeltsin standing here in the Rose Garden, and we entered into a deal to eliminate the biggest and most threatening ballistic missiles . . . and it was almost, "Ho-hum, what have you done for me recently?" '

Circumlocution does not always come in such generous helpings. It is more likely to pop up phrase by phrase. A police officer may prefer *an explosive device*, or even *an infernal machine*, to a *bomb*. *Except* is also frequently contorted into *with the exception of*.

The words *nature* and *character* do heavy circumlocutory duty: *inquiries of a delicate nature/ character* – when *delicate inquiries* is enough. Or *items of a suspect nature will be removed and destroyed* – for *suspect items*.

Well embedded in poor English usage are *with reference to* . . . *with regard to* . . . *with respect to* . . . when the writer need only say *about*.

Circumlocutionist's lexicon

As to whether (whether)
as yet (yet)
at the time of writing (now/at present)
at this moment in time (now/at present)
avail ourselves of the privilege of (accept)

Consequent upon (because of)
consonant with (agreeing/suiting/matching)
could hardly be less propitious (is bad/unfortunate/ unpromising)

During such time as (while)
during the course of the day (during the day)

Facts, facts, facts!
apart from the fact that (because/since/although)
because of the fact that (because)
by virtue of the fact that (because)
due to the fact that (because)
in the light of the fact that (because)
irrespective of the fact that (although)
notwithstanding the fact that (even though/if)
on account of the fact that (because)
owing to the fact that (because)
regardless of the fact that (although)

Few in number (few)
for the very good reason that (because)

Give up on (give up)
go in to bat for (defend/represent/help)

I beg to differ (disagree)
in accordance with your instructions (acting on/
following)
in accordance with the regulations (under)
in addition to which (besides)
in all probability (probably)
in anticipation of (expecting)
inasmuch as (because)
in association with (with)
in close proximity to (near)
in consequence of (because of)
in contention (competing)
in contradistinction to (compared to/with)
in connection with (about)
in excess of (over/more than)
in favour of (for, or, with a cheque, to)
in less than no time (soon/quickly)
in more than one instance (more than once)
in many instances (often)

33

in no time at all (quickly)
in respect of (about/concerning)
in the absence of (without)
in the context of (for/considering)
in the near future (soon)
in the recent past (recently)
in the vicinity (near/nearby)
in view of (because of)

Large in stature (large/big)

Nothing if not (very)

Not, not! Who's there?

The double negative is usually confusing. But it is occasionally useful.

The bomb attack was not unexpected.

If you lived in a terrorist-ridden area, where to be bombed sooner or later was no great surprise, *not unexpected* would convey a suspended kind of expectation better than *was expected* or *was no surprise*.

Generally, though, the double negative is pompous and needlessly confusing:

The Prime Minister is not unmindful of the damage already suffered . . .
The company proposes a not-ungenerous compensation payment . . .

Of a high order (high/great/considerable)
of the opinion that (think/believe)
on a temporary basis (temporary/temporarily)
on the ground that (because)
on the part of (by)

34

Prior to (before)

Subsequent to (after)

To the best of my knowledge and belief (as far as I know/I believe)
to the extent that (if)

With a view to (to)
with reference to (about)
with regard to (about)
with respect to (about/concerning)

Tautology

Free gift! Added extra! Added bonus!

Exciting claims. Wasted words. All examples of
tautology – the use of more than one word to convey
the same thought.

A gift, if not free, is not a gift – except in the slang
usage 'That car was an absolute gift at £3,000'.

Something *extra* is clearly something *added*. And a
bonus is normally an *addition*. Even if the word is used
to describe something apart from money, an *added
bonus* is an *added addition*. Nonsense, obviously. Yet
we hear and read *added bonus* every day, from people
who have not thought what they are saying, or do not
care.

Tautologist's lexicon

absolute certainty (certainty)
added bonus (bonus)
added extra (extra)
quite/very/markedly distinct (distinct)
each and every (each/every)
end result (result)
following an earlier incident – public transport
announcements about delays (following an accident)
forward planning (planning)
future plans (plans)
future prospects (prospects)
free gift (gift)
past history (past/history)
really excellent (excellent)
revert back (revert/return/go back)

Quite so

Perfect. Excellent. Unique.

These are words that cannot be qualified. A vase is either perfect or it is not. It cannot be *better* than perfect. So *quite perfect*, *absolutely perfect* are tautologies. The same goes for *excellent*.

Unique means *the only one of its kind*. You can't get much more unique than that. Not even *quite unique* or *absolutely/utterly unique*.

Witter Words: Dump Your Witter in the Bin

The language is sprinkled with Witter Words –
expressions that clog a sentence and add nothing to the
information or meaning. In this, Witter Words differ
from circumlocution, which certainly adds
information, but adds it in the wrong order, holding
back the main point.

In our elaborate Victorian death notice for the Rev.
A.M. Bennett (see p. 30) the reader has to plod through
53 words before arriving at 'breathed his last'. But those
53 words tell us the place and time of death, how long
he had been vicar, the name of the church, the extent
of his influence and the reaction in the parish to news
of his death.

Witter Words, on the other hand, tell us nothing.
Some are more often heard in speech, especially among
the prattlers of radio and television. But many appear
in writing.

Witter warning list

As it were
As such – as in *the rules, as such, do not preclude* . . .
Often mistakenly used where the writer would do
better to say *the rules, by themselves* or *the rules, alone*
. . . carrying the implication that however limited the
strict rules, there is some other obligation to consider.

By and large
By definition

Funnily/strangely/oddly/curiously enough

Having said that

I am here to tell you
38

I am the first to admit
If you like – as in *he was, if you like, a rebel*
I have to say, here and now
In a manner of speaking
In point of fact
It goes without saying

Let me just say, right here and now
Let's just be clear about this

Needless to say

Quite simply – as in *quite simply, they are starving*

Shall I say – as in *it is, shall I say, a novel approach*
So to speak

The fact of the matter – as in *the fact of the matter is, the Government were wrong*. Generally used by a politician for *the claim I hope to get away with* . . .

Unless and until – as in *unless and until they pay, there will be no more food for them*. The *unless* is not needed. *Until* makes the necessary condition.

When all is said and done – as in *when all is said and done, we came out on top*. Not entirely meaningless, but perhaps better replaced with *still/however/nevertheless*. With all due respect/the greatest respect
Within the foreseeable future

Here is a sentence which includes three Witter phrases:

> *Needless to say*, we are, *if you like*, facing difficulties which, *when all is said and done*, we did not create ourselves.

The sheer lack of meaning in those phrases becomes

more obvious when we find we can move them around the sentence, to no effect:

> We are, *if you like*, facing difficulties which, *needless to say*, *when all is said and done*, we did not create ourselves.

Or:

> *When all is said and done*, we are, *if you like*, facing difficulties which, *needless to say*, we did not create ourselves.

All those extra Witter Words, just to say:

> We are facing difficulties which we did not create ourselves.

Saying it ever so nicely

They are called euphemisms: words and phrases with which people avoid making a statement that is direct, clear and honest.

A euphemism is often used out of kindness, when the direct expression might give needless offence. For example a deaf person may be described as *hard of hearing*, a part-blind person as *partially sighted*.

This is taken to an absurd extreme with ultra-euphemisms such as *visually* or *aurally challenged*.

Poor people are *in a lower income bracket* or *under-privileged*. Their slum homes are *inner city areas of deprivation*. When the city decides to clear away its slums, the process is called *urban renewal*, rather than slum clearance.

If part of a city has people from a variety of racial backgrounds, the result is an *ethnic mix* of citizens, any of whom may be proud of his or her *ethnicity*.

Euphemisms abound, and have done for centuries,

when sex is discussed. Adultery was once *criminal conversation*. When lovers met, it was highly likely that *intimacy occurred*. The human body in particular has attracted the euphemists. *Winkle, willy, John Thomas, Percy, todger* and *tool* are only a few of the euphemisms for the male organ; for the female, *pussy, fanny* or simply *down below*. A facetious person might call his backside *my nether regions*. And someone seeking a sex-change operation will find it is called *gender reassignment*.

If the surgeon is *the worse for wear* or *a bit merry*, or has *taken a drop to drink*, a slip of the scalpel may turn the patient into a dead person – *the dear departed*. The body is handed over to a *funeral director*, who will still be unable to shake off the traditional expression, undertaker. Any unwanted belongings will be carted away by a *refuse collector* or *cleansing operative* – whose Old Man would have been a plain dustman.

At the inquest on the departed, someone may allow a false impression to be given, by holding back information – being *economical with the truth*. If the patient's body is lost, somewhere between funeral parlour and graveyard, embarrassing publicity may be dealt with by the undertakers' *corporate public relations director*, or *publicity manager*. The *customer liaison assistant* whose mistake led to the re-routing of the corpse is likely to be subjected by his *Director of Human Resources*, formerly personnel manager, to *outplacement* – the sack.

This news may well drive the customer liaison assistant on an urgent *call of nature* to the *Gents, loo, WC* or *Little Boys' Room*, where once stood the lavatory. A female assistant, of course, would choose the *powder room*, or *Ladies*. (An American is likely to talk of *visiting the bathroom*, even when referring to the family dog's use of a lamp-post.)

A Bit of a Muddle

Muddled writing occurs when the author is not really thinking about what he or she is putting on paper.

Disaster at lunchtime

> The lunch hour is not what it appears to be for the majority of workers.
>
> An hour is more likely to be fewer than 30 minutes for two in every five workers, while a mere 5 per cent take a more leisurely attitude and admit to exceeding the traditional time limit.
>
> *The Independent*

An apparent attempt at being jokey turns the first part of paragraph two into a muddle of statistics likely to dissuade the reader from finishing the sentence.

Mixing ordinary figures with percentages is another irritation: the reader has to stop and work out how the two sets compare. Perhaps the passage can be rescued, though:

> For 40 in 100 workers, that 'hour' is likely to be under 30 minutes. Only five in 100 take a more leisurely attitude and admit to exceeding the traditional time limit.

A nasty mess in the vestibule

> The high for the day was achieved for a marble Georgian chimney-piece circa 1770 with superbly carved tablets of Diana and her hounds.
>
> It went on estimate for £23,650 to Bartlett, the Bermondsey dealer in architectural fittings who paid £330 for three piles of marble at Castle Howard last

year which he has since sold to America for about
£150,000, reconstructed as a 15ft vestibule by Sir
John Vanbrugh.

Daily Telegraph auction report from the Duke of
Westminster's Eaton Hall estate in Cheshire.

A thorough mess, isn't it? Ignoring the jargonaut's *high*
in the first sentence (see *Jargonaut's Lexicon*, p. 23),
we are violently wrenched from the latest doings of
Bermondsey Bartlett to an entirely different event, year
and place.

What exactly was it that Bartlett from Bermondsey
sold to America? The marble? Castle Howard? Last
year itself? And what exactly was *reconstructed as a 15ft
vestibule by Sir John Vanbrugh*? Marble? Castle
Howard?

And wasn't Sir John Vanbrugh, by then, rather old
to be reconstructing anything, being already 62 when
he officially died in 1726?

By cheating a little and looking at a reference book,
we see that Sir John was an architect as well as a
playwright. Castle Howard, in Yorkshire, was the first
building he designed. So could it be that the *three piles
of marble* had originally been a 15ft vestibule which he
designed? Let us assume so. Let us also assume that
sold to America does not mean *sold to the United States
government*.

It now becomes possible, with heavy lifting-gear and
wearing our hard hats, to reconstruct this pile of
literary rubble – not, perhaps, as a grand 15ft vestibule,
but at least as a piece of clear English.

It went at the estimated price, £23,650, to Bartlett,
the Bermondsey dealer in architectural fittings. Last
year, at Castle Howard, the same dealer paid £330
for three piles of marble, originally a 15ft vestibule
by the castle's architect, Sir John Vanbrugh. Bartlett has since sold the marble in America for

£150,000. It has been used to reconstruct the vestibule.

And not a scrap of valuable verbal marble vandalised.

After the smart card, the smart book

> This passbook is required by the Society when
> making a withdrawal.
>
> Building Society notice

What a clever little book, able to make its own
withdrawals. Perhaps the Society has a special aversion
to the words *you* and *must*. Otherwise the wording could
have been simpler, clearer and more direct –

> You must show this passbook to withdraw money.

To visit, or not to visit

> Trust staff, the report discloses, have been advised
> that they should only visit the area after midday in
> the event of an emergency.

That snippet could mean:

> Trust staff have been advised that if there is an
> emergency, they should not visit the area in the
> morning.

It could also mean:

> Trust staff have been advised that the only time to
> visit the area is after midday – and even then, only
> if there is an emergency.

That word *only* is part of the problem. Pedants have

always fretted about the correct placing of the word. In this example, they would be right to fret. Does the writer mean *only visit that area*? Or *visit that area only after midday*? Or *visit after midday only if there is an emergency*?

The other part of the problem is the piece of verbiage, *in the event of*, meaning, in clearer English, *if there is* or *unless there is* an emergency.

What the sentence so clumsily failed to convey was this:

> Trust staff have been advised not to visit the area after midday, unless there is an emergency.

Doorstep body horror

This absurdity, taken from a newspaper, is a masterpiece of muddle:

> A Texan undertaker left the body of a man on the doorstep of his son because he could not afford a cremation.

Apart from the pen-of-my-aunt construction – whose son owned the doorstep? The dead man's son? The undertaker's son? – who could not afford a cremation? The dead man? His son? The undertaker?

At first sight, this dreadful sentence is easy to rewrite without confusion or loss of fact. But try doing it also without repetition, which the writer may have been desperate to avoid:

> A Texan undertaker dumped a dead man on the man's son's doorstep because the son could not afford a cremation.

Clumsy, as well as repetitive.

> A dead man was dumped on his son's doorstep by

a Texan undertaker because the son could not afford a cremation.

Still repetitive.

A dead man whose son could not afford a cremation was dumped on the son's doorstep . . .

Yet again, repetitive.

Just one more heave:

A Texan undertaker who found that a dead man's family could not afford a cremation dumped the body on the son's doorstep.

It is taking no great liberty to introduce the word *family*, and in this context *the* son is normal usage.

Like as not

Lazy (or ignorant) use of *like* can change the writer's intended meaning:

Like the Heath administration more than 20 years ago, the miners have weakened a Tory government's authority.

Now, it is possible – even likely – that a government would weaken itself by sheer cackhandedness. But that is obviously not what the writer wanted to say. It is the *miners* who are alleged to have weakened governmental authority on both occasions. Replace *like* by *as with*, and the problem is solved.

Like is also widely misused to introduce examples:

It included stars like Frank Sinatra, Bob Hope and Michael Jackson.

Were these mere lookalikes? Or do we really mean stars *such as*? It is lucky, since this misuse is so common, that it rarely causes misunderstanding.

Might or may

Misuse of *may* instead of *might* is common and can confuse. *May* is correct when an outcome of fact is still unknown. *Might* is right when an *if* is lurking in the background – when we discuss something that was likely or possible on some past occasion.

RIGHT: If it had not been for the police, I might have died. (But I didn't.)
WRONG: If it had not been for the police, I may have died.

RIGHT: I accept that I may have been mistaken. (I am still not sure.)
WRONG: I accept that I might have been mistaken.

RIGHT: It might have been a mistake to turn right, so I didn't. (At the time, I wasn't sure.)
WRONG: It might have been a mistake to turn right, because I hit another car.

RIGHT: It may have been a mistake, but I turned right. (I still don't know it if was a mistake or not.)
WRONG: It may have been a mistake to turn right, so I didn't.

Overloading can Sink a Sentence

Consider this passage from the *Daily Telegraph*:

> Seven of the 33 buildings in St James's Square, in the heart of one of the most expensive parts of the West End, display For Sale or To Let signs.

Nothing wrong there. But then:

> The sight of some of the capital's most exclusive business addresses languishing empty – when not long ago they were snapped up as corporate headquarters – brings home the impact of the recession as financial controllers cut costs by letting out spare space vacated by staff who have been made redundant or exiled to less costly locations.

Now, readers of 'quality' newspapers may be perfectly able to wind their way through that sentence. But why should they have to?

Let us count the items of information that the author has loaded in:

1: some of the capital's most exclusive business addresses
2: are empty
3: when not long ago they were snapped up
4: as corporate headquarters
5: impact of the recession
6: financial controllers cutting costs
7: by letting out spare space
8: . . . which was left empty when staff either were made redundant
9: or were moved
10: to somewhere cheaper

Clearly, the structure ought to be dismantled and

reassembled in more manageable form. The major pieces of information are: (a) The situation is caused by an economic recession; (b) The recession meant that offices were emptied because staff were sacked or moved to cheaper accommodation; (c) Companies also saved money by renting out offices they used to occupy themselves.

What could the author have done instead? If we indulge his taste for *languishing* buildings, he could have written:

> The sight of some of the capital's most exclusive business addresses languishing empty brings home the impact of the recession. Offices have been left empty as staff were made redundant, or moved to cheaper accommodation. Financial controllers have cut costs by letting out the space their companies no longer need.

Sentence under the cosh

The same newspaper carried a less formidable, but nevertheless overloaded, opening paragraph:

> A man living alone was attacked by seven armed robbers who forced him at gunpoint to open the front door of his secluded country cottage before leaving him so badly beaten that he is now afraid to return home.

To cure this, we need help from the second paragraph:

> Mr __, a former England Boys rugby player who weighs 22 stones, was returning to his home in __, Kent, on Thursday from his nearby garden furniture company when the gang struck . . .

49

The main news points seem to be: (a) A man was badly beaten by robbers in his secluded cottage; (b) He was beaten so badly that he is now afraid to return home – presumably from hospital. The additional facts, that there were seven robbers, that they were armed, that they forced him at gunpoint to open the front door, can wait a moment.

The opening paragraph could have read:

> A man living alone in a secluded cottage was beaten so badly by armed robbers that he is afraid to go home. Seven armed men struck as he approached the house, and forced him at gunpoint to open his front door.

In danger of decomposing

From another newspaper, the *Independent*, comes this:

> Cage studied for a time with Schoenberg, in Los Angeles, and electing to follow the Viennese composer's path as opposed to the Stravinskyan alternative available in the 1930s, but finding he had none of the harmonic sense which Schoenberg deemed fundamental to musical structure, he set himself up as primarily a percussion composer interested in the pure unfolding of time and, subsequently, in the pure operation of chance.

Even though this obituary was addressed to people who know their musicians, the sentence still seems to pack in more information than the reader should have to cope with, in one gulp.

Let's break it up, inserting the occasional comma for extra clarity:

> Cage studied for a time with Schoenberg, in Los Angeles, and elected to follow the Viennese compos-

er's path, as opposed to the Stravinskyan alternative available in the 1930s. Finding he had none of the harmonic sense which Schoenberg deemed fundamental to musical structure, he set himself up as primarily a percussion composer, interested in the pure unfolding of time and, subsequently, in the pure operation of chance.

These slight amendments may still not make the passage comprehensible to those of us who don't know much about that corner of the musical world. But at least they offer a better chance of getting to the end.

Danger: Here be Clichés

Many favourite phrases which once added colour to the language have been worked far too hard, over the years. We all drift into using them: some people can hardly manage a sentence without a cliché or two.

You don't have to give up all clichés for ever: sometimes the hackneyed phrase is the neatest way of expressing yourself. But before plunging on with your cliché, ask yourself: Are you sure? Or might a quick rewrite avoid the need for it?

If you make up your mind to watch out for creeping clichés and ration them, you will be surprised how easy it becomes to do without – and how much fresher your writing becomes as a result.

Here are a few to watch for:

Abdicating our responsibilities
accidentally on purpose
according to plan
act of contrition
acid test
add insult to injury
all at sea
all in the same boat
all over bar the shouting
all things considered
almost too good to be true
arms of Morpheus
angel of mercy
angry silence
as luck/fate would have it
as sure as eggs is eggs
at the end of the day
at this point in time
at your peril
auspicious occasion
avid reader

Bad omens
bag and baggage
ball and chain (marital)
barometer of the economy
bat an eyelid
batten down the hatches
battle lines being drawn
beavering away
between a rock and a hard place
between the Devil and the deep blue sea
beware the Greek bearing gifts
(the) bird has flown
bit of a bombshell
blanket coverage
bleed them white
blind drunk
blind leading the blind
blinkered view
blissful harmony
blissful ignorance
(my) blood boiled
blood out of a stone
bloody but unbowed
blot on the landscape
blow the whistle
(it) bodes ill
bored to death
(the) bubble burst
borrowed time
brought to book
bruising battle/encounter
bumper-to-bumper traffic jams
burden of proof
but I digress

Call of the wild
call the shots/tune
callow youth
calm before the storm

came in from the cold
camp as a row of tents
captive audience
card up his sleeve
cards stacked against
cardinal sin
carrot-and-stick treatment
carte blanche
cast of thousands
cast the first stone
(given a) clean bill of health
catalogue of misfortune/misery
cat among the pigeons
Catch-22 situation
catholic taste
caustic comment
cautious optimism
centre of his universe
chain of events
(as different as) chalk and cheese
chapter and verse
cherished belief
chew the cud
chew the fat
chip off the old block
chop and change
chorus of approval/disapproval
chosen few
come to the crunch
complete and utter candour
compulsive viewing
conspicuous by his absence
consummation devoutly to be wished
cool as a cucumber
cool, calm and collected
copious notes
crack of dawn
crisis of confidence
cup of sorrow runneth over

current climate
cut any ice

Damn with faint praise
Dark Continent
dark horse
dark secret
deadly accurate
deafening silence
deaf to entreaties
deep gloom
depths of depravity
despite misgivings
devour every word
dicing with death
dirty raincoat brigade
doom and gloom merchants
drives me up the wall
(wearing the) Dunce's cap

Eagerly devour
enjoy the fleshpots
eternal regret
(to my) eternal shame
eternally in your/my/their debt
evening of our lives
every man jack of them
every stage of the game

Face the music
fair sex
feed the Inner Man
few and far between
(the) final insult
fine-tooth comb
finger in every pie
finger of suspicion
fit as a fiddle
follow like sheep

fond belief
fraught with danger/peril
frenzy of activity
fresh fields and pastures new
fudge the issue

Generous to a fault
gentle giant
gentler sex
glowing tribute
golden opportunity
go to the ends of the earth
green with envy
ground to a halt
guardian angel

Hand-to-mouth existence
happy accident
happy medium
happily/comfortably ensconced
having said that
heaping ridicule
heart and soul
hell hath no fury
(come) hell or high water
high and dry
hit the panic button
hive of activity
Hobson's choice
hoist with his own petard
horns of a dilemma
horses for courses
howling gale/tempest

Ill-gotten gains
ill-starred venture
(the) impossible dream
inch-by-inch search
inordinate amount of

(one/not one) iota
it seemed an eternity
it will all end in tears
I must fly

Just not on

Keep your head above water
keep your own counsel
knocked into a cocked hat

Lack-lustre performance
large as life
lavish ceremony/banquet/hospitality/praise
leave no stone unturned
leave no avenue unexplored
level playing-field
lick his wounds
little local difficulty
little the wiser
living in the Dark Ages
long arm of the law
long hot summer
lost cause
lost in admiration
lost in contemplation
love you and leave you

Made of sterner stuff
make a killing
man of straw
method in his madness
Midas touch
(the) mind boggles
mixed blessing (worse still, not an unmixed blessing –
see *Circumlocution*, p. 30)
(a) model of its kind
more honoured in the breach than in the observance
more in sorrow than in anger

more sinned against than sinning
mortgaged up to the hilt
move the goalposts
much-needed reforms

Necessity is the mother of invention
no peace for the wicked
not a scrap of evidence
not to put too fine a point upon it

Offer he couldn't refuse
older and wiser
olive branch
one fell swoop
operative word
own worst enemy

Package of measures
painstaking investigation
palpable nonsense
part and parcel
path of virtue
pinpoint accuracy
plain as a pikestaff
plain as the nose on your face
poison/ed chalice
pomp and circumstance
press on regardless
prime candidate
pure as the driven snow
(when/if) push comes to shove

Resounding silence
rings a bell
roll out the red carpet
rose between two thorns
(one) rotten apple in a barrel
ruffled feathers
58

Sale of the century
search high and low
seething cauldron
set in stone
shake the dust from their feet
shot across the bows
simmering hatred
skin of our teeth
snatch defeat from the jaws of victory
snatch victory from the jaws of defeat
solid as a rock
sorely needed
splendid isolation
spoken for
standing ovation
stick to our guns
steady as a rock
stir up a hornets' nest
straight and narrow
strain every nerve
strange as it may seem
strange to relate
strapping great fellow
straw that broke the camel's back
strike a chord
stuff and nonsense
suffer in silence
suffer fools gladly
sugar the pill

Tarred with the same brush
technological wizardry
tender mercies
there, but for the grace of God
this day and age
thunderous applause
time flies
time heals all ills/wounds
time waits for no man

(in a) time warp
tip of the iceberg
tireless campaigner/crusader
tissue of lies
to all intents and purposes
to my dying day
to my utter chagrin
too awful/terrible/horrible to contemplate
too many cooks
torrential rain
towering inferno
tower of strength

Utter bilge
ultra-sophisticated
(take an) unconscionable time
unequal task
up to his neck in debt/in it

Wages of sin
wash my hands of it
(all) water under the bridge
wealth of evidence/experience/knowledge/material
wedded bliss
welter of evidence
wheels within wheels
whisked to hospital
(idea/man/political party) whose time has come
winter of discontent
with a vengeance
without a shadow of doubt
without fear of contradiction
wringing of hands

What's your cliché rating?

How many from that list are you aware of having
written lately?
60

More than ten? If there were such a thing as a cliché-holic, it would be you. If your job involves much writing, someone in the office is probably making a secret collection of your greatest excesses. Study the list again. Then promise yourself a thorough cliché clear-out.

Between five and ten? You're not a hopeless case – yet. But do run the cliché detector over your next piece of writing before you let anyone else see it.

Up to five? Not so bad – but don't slacken. If five clichés can get past you, so can six, seven . . . and before you know it, you'll be standing in Cliché Corner *wearing the Dunce's Cap* (see list).

Not one? Almost (as the cliché would have it) too good to be true. But if you're sure you are not even slightly cheating, congratulations on helping to keep the English language fresh and alive.

Complete the cliché
How many of these well-worn expressions can you complete with the missing word?
(Answers below)

1. a gift from the . . . .
2. . . . . scepticism
3. . . . . averted
4. like peas in a . . .
5. . . . . . savage
6. light at the end of the . . . . . .
7. overweening . . . . ./. . . . .
8. blown off . . . . . .
9. address the . . . . .

Awfully Abstract: Soggy Words for Soggy People

An abstract noun represents nothing of substance. Using one can knock the stuffing out of what you are trying to say. There is nothing wrong with the words themselves. They all originally meant something. *Aspect*, for example, is correctly used to mean *way of looking* at a subject: *When viewed from the aspect of England's interests, it was unsatisfactory.*

But when the word is used to mean *part* or *consideration*, your sentence suddenly becomes soggy: *We had to consider the money aspect.*

Sogginess is the general effect of the Awful Abstract. Here are some of the abstract nouns and adjective/ adverb phrases to be found crawling all over the language nowadays . . .

(in) abeyance (suspended)

abrogation (breach/rejection/spurning)

amenity, as in *the school has gymnasium and swimming amenities* (gymnasium and swimming pool)

aspect, as in *the major aspect of the plan* (the important part of the plan)

attitude, as in *he adopted a menacing attitude* (he looked menacing)

availability, as in *supplies will be subject to limited availability* (supplies will be limited/scarce)

basis, as in *he worked on a part-time basis* (he worked part-time). The word can sensibly be used when it *means* basis: a foundation, beginning or main ingredient. (*He marshalled his troops on the basis of a spy's information/ the basis of their romance was a shared love of music/ the basis of her pudding was bread.*)

capability/capacity, as in *they have a chemical warfare capability/capacity* (they have chemical weapons)

cessation, as in *a cessation of hostilities was hoped for* (it was hoped hostilities would cease/stop/end)

character, as in *the parcel was of a suspect character* (the parcel was suspect)

degree, as in *she showed a considerable degree of restraint* (she showed considerable restraint)

description, as in *they had no plan of any description* (they had no plan)

desirability, as in *he questioned the desirability of the proposals* (he asked whether the proposals were desirable)

degree, as in *he displayed a high degree of courage* (great courage)

element, as in *there was a rebel element* (there were rebels)

expectation, as in *expectation of jam tomorrow was expressed by the government* (the government expected jam tomorrow)

factor, as in *remember the unemployment factor* (remember unemployment)

feature – see *aspect*

function, as in *following a complete review of the Greater Manchester Police Press and Public Relations Function* (review of Greater Manchester Press and Public Relations)

level, as in *the general level of conduct was unsatisfactory* (in general/generally, conduct was unsatisfactory)

manner, as in *he drove in a reckless manner* (drove recklessly)

nature, as in *arrangements of a temporary nature* (temporary arrangements) *operation*, as in *these lifts are not in operation* (not working)

participation, as in *there was enthusiastic participation on the part of the members* (the members took part enthusiastically)

persuasion, as in *he was of the Methodist persuasion* (he was a Methodist)

situation, as in *please let me know the present state of the situation* (please let me know how things are)

Sharpen Up Your Memos

Writing to an old friend, or your grandmother, you can ramble as much as you like – just as you might on a cheap-rate phone call.

Business correspondence, of course, is a different matter. You need to be succinct and to get to the main point or points straight away.

Let's imagine you have to tell your boss that a pet project of his has not gone entirely as planned. The bad news is bound to irritate him anyway. And his irritation will not be soothed by having to hunt through a wordy preamble before he stumbles across it.

How not to tell it

You instructed me to organise a 'Knees-up' in a Brewery, to celebrate the 100th anniversary of Hardboiled Eggs plc.

I was asked to approach certain local brewery companies with a view to establishing whether one or other of them would be able to accommodate our function on one or other of our preferred dates, bearing in mind that it has to be held as close as possible to Founder's Day, Friday, February the 13th.

My first inquiry was to Messrs WhatBrew, of Staggering Way, the closest to our own offices. In principle, they were keenly interested, but on checking their bookings for similar events were regretfully forced to conclude that none of our required dates was available, though they certainly hoped to be able to be of service on some future occasion.

I next contacted Messrs Tallyho Breweries, of Stumbling Lane – rather further afield but with an excellent reputation for organising these affairs.

Unfortunately, it appears that they no longer do them, owing to difficulties in obtaining damage and injury insurance for events involving stockbrokers and Rugby players (it was thought commercially unwise to be seen to discriminate against these particular groups).

This left, in practice, only the much smaller firm of Messrs Tipsy & Droppitt, of Hiccups Corner, mentioned in conference by one of the sales force. After several fruitless efforts to contact this brewery, I learned that in fact, as recently as the middle of last summer, they went into liquidation, as a result of the Chief Accountant leaving his wife and five children in order to abscond to Latin America with a considerable sum of his company's VAT money and the MD's third wife (the MD being a hopeless alcoholic).

It unfortunately appears that unless we are prepared to go a good deal further afield for our Knees-up, there is likely to be considerable difficulty in adhering to your original plan.

You may wish to call another conference, or perhaps we could discuss privately any alternative suggestions.

No doubt the boss would be intrigued by the bits of gossip you have picked up during your research. But not when it gets in the way of the main point: What progress with the Knees-up Plan?

By the time the boss got to the fairly muted confession, he or she would have been foaming like a pint of hot WhatBrew's Special XXX, and the writer clearing his desk within the hour.

Much better, then, to come clean from the start.

The quick (and nearly painless) way

> Our plan for a Founder's Day Knees-up in a brewery has run into a difficulty.

> Of the three breweries a reasonable distance from our offices, one cannot offer any of our suggested dates, on or near Friday, February 13th; another no longer does such functions and the third has gone out of business.

If you feel a little cringeing might be in order over your failure to deliver, you could add:

> I am sorry I have not been able to carry out your instructions. Perhaps we could discuss other possibilities.

The same get-it-over-with approach also applies if you find you have to put a proposal which you know the boss will not like – or even when you have *good* news!

Making it look good

A long letter or memo – assuming all those words really are necessary – can be made less forbidding if you break it up with simple tricks of layout.

It is common enough to give a main subject heading –

PROPOSED FOUNDER'S DAY
BREWERY KNEES-UP

But you can also break up the slab of text under it with subheadings, preferably at the side –

Why the plan has not worked

> WhatBrew, of Staggering Way, could not offer any of our suggested dates . . .

Or inset, like this –

> **Why the plan has not worked**   WhatBrew, of Staggering Way, cannot offer any of our required dates

Another way to put a bit of air into your memo would be an extra bit of display, using asterisks or 'bullets' – full stops, the bigger the better (see *Wonders of the Word Processor*, p. 95).

> Of the three breweries I was told to contact –
> * One could not manage any of our required dates
> * Another no longer does these events
> * The third has gone out of business

Sometimes it may be useful to number your sub-sections, though this can look boring.

Sum up to start with

It is often a good idea to start your long missive – one that runs to more than a single page – with a short, sharp summary of the most important points. Make sure you don't leave out something vital: your busy boss might just rely on the summary to keep up with what is happening, and so miss that important point.

Although our Brewery Knees-up message is not long enough to need a summary, let us stick to it for our example.

> PROPOSED FOUNDER'S DAY
> BREWERY KNEES-UP
>
> * We are unable to use any of the three breweries discussed.
> * No other brewery is within reasonable distance of our offices.
> * Should we discuss what else to do?

Having summarised, take care, in expanding your points, to do it in the same order.

Dear Sir, Please find enclosed some nonsense

When writing to someone outside your office – a customer, for example – keep in mind that, hectic though the pace in your business may seem, the person you are writing to is likely to have no more time to waste than you have.

This was a letter from a building society, about a passbook which a customer had accidentally left at its office:

> I write to confirm that I have enclosed your passbook which was left at our Branch today.

> I trust that this is in order, and if I can be of any further assistance, please do not hesitate to contact me.

What a relief to recover the missing passbook! And what a polite letter! And how devoid of genuine thought!

In the first paragraph *I write to confirm that* is meaningless, if there has been no previous discussion of the matter.

I have enclosed is an odd way to say *I enclose* – or even, to defy tradition, *Here is*.

The initial capital for Branch might be office style, and doesn't get in the way of the meaning, but is unnecessary.

This passage easily comes down to:

> I enclose your passbook which was left at our branch today.

The second paragraph, in the circumstances, is pointless. What might *not* be *in order*? Is the customer

likely to protest at the return of his passbook? And
what *further assistance* can be rendered, concerning the
book – unless perhaps the customer discovers
unexplained withdrawals of his money?

That second paragraph wastes the time of both writer
and reader. It can go.

In this word-processor age, it would be a good idea
to make sure that even if the computer is to churn out
automated letters, the text has some bearing on the
subject.

Don't let the machines take over!

Your opening shot

There is no logical reason to start a letter, whether
business or personal, with the word Dear. But the
habit is so ingrained that if you began with a blunt *Mr
Smith* you would be considered rude. It would have a
Now look here . . . tone. So perhaps the Dear custom
is not one to abandon.

And how do we proceed after that?

Replying to somebody's letter, a businessman or
woman will generally refer to it at once. Very practical,
too. But some people go about it in an incredibly
clumsy, stilted style.

We are in receipt of your letter . . .

Your letter of 13th February is hereby acknow-
ledged . . .

We are obliged for your communication of . . .

This letter is by way of reply to yours of . . .

All more satisfactorily expressed, as so many people
fortunately do, with *Thank you for your letter*.

Making the above examples even more gruesome,
occasionally, are the terrible twins, *inst.* (for *instant*,

meaning this month) and *ult.* (for *ultimo*, meaning last month).

Given the dwindling number of Latin scholars carrying on business today, there is no real demand for either of these.

And finally . . . the sign-off

None of the usual business-letter sign-offs makes much sense, from the simple *yours faithfully, yours truly* or *yours sincerely* to the archaic flourish of *I beg to remain, your Obedient Servant.*

Another form from the foggy past is: *We would be grateful if you would be kind enough to reply/supply the information/settle this account/ at your earliest convenience, and oblige . . .*

Even if the letter is some sort of threat, *and oblige* . . . has an enfeebling effect: the snivelling tone of an anxious tailor beseeching the Squire to pay at least a little something . . .

But why do we use even the simpler sign-offs? Answer: they're there because they're there. And even today, it would seem a little brusque, even impolite, not to put *something* between your letter and your signature.

So how do we decide which is the more suitable form? Once, the rough-and-ready rule was that if you got a letter ending *Yours faithfully*, you adopted the same style in your reply. And similarly with other sign-offs.

Of the three basic insincere sign-offs, *Yours sincerely* is obviously the warmest-sounding. *Yours truly* is probably the most meaningless. There seems no harm in continuing *Yours faithfully/sincerely*. But use *sincerely* only if you are addressing someone by his or her name, not as Dear Sir/s. *Best wishes* or *Kind regards* also still have their place, when you want to add a flicker of warmth.

You may of course want to be the pioneer who dispenses with all of them.

In which case, jolly good luck – but check with the boss first (unless you *are* the boss).

Letters From Home

Domestic matters that in the past were dealt with by letter are often disposed of nowadays by a quick phone call. But there are still occasions when a letter is better. And at those times, you will usually need to express yourself as clearly as possible . . .

To the council, about a pavement

> Dear Sirs: It's an absolutely bloody disgrace that anybody could leave things until they get in such a state! ! !
>
> I've very nearly broken a leg several times tripping over it and one poor old soul a couple of doors down is terrified to even step outside any more, in a manner of speaking, since her tumble last month (I'm talking about the pavements that you have let go to rack and ruin for the last 18 months, if a day.)
>
> Wake up, can't you, and get something done around here before there's a really serious tragedy. And I warn you, if it's me, I shall sue! ! !

That, of course, is how not to do it. The greatest weakness of the letter, as a complaint demanding action, is that it does not explain at once what the writer is fuming about.

However angry you may be about something, let off steam by kicking the dustbin over – but keep your letter cool and factual. Imagine that this is an office matter, and use the restraint you would feel obliged to exercise in making a business complaint.

TRY THIS INSTEAD

Dear Sirs:

Dangerous Pavement

The paving outside this house and several others is broken and dangerous.

I have stumbled on it several times and at least one other resident, an old lady, is afraid to risk walking on the pavement for fear of an acccident.

Will you please get the paving repaired, urgently.

To a magistrates' court, about a parking fine

You'd have thought there was enough real crime going on in our streets without the long arm of the law wasting time picking off innocent motorists like this.

I told the silly bitch I'd broken down but she still went ahead and wrote the ticket out. What was I supposed to do? Sling a ton of saloon car over one shoulder and hike it off to a garage?

If you think I'm paying good money after that, you are fooling yourselves.

I want this ticket cancelled, not be hauled into court to explain why, because I can't afford the time off work and this letter ought to be good enough explanation for anybody.

As with the broken-pavement letter, this complaint lets the routine jibe about police work get in the way of the real point: the writer feels it unfair that a parking ticket was issued in the circumstances described.

The abusive tone does not help. There is nothing novel about an indignant motorist: the average driver is born indignant. At best, your justifiable spleen will be shrugged off: at worst, it will annoy an official who might otherwise have sympathised.

I enclose a parking ticket which I believe should not have been issued to me.

The ticket was put on my car, in my presence, at the corner of Smith Street and Brown Street, on Friday October 7 at 10.05 a.m. At the time, as I explained to the parking warden, my car had broken down.

I would have liked to contest the case in court, but cannot afford to take time off work to do so.

However, I hope you will agree that, in the circumstances, the ticket was unfairly issued and should be cancelled.

To a noisy neighbour

I'm fed up hammering on the bedroom wall till my knuckles hurt and this noise has got to stop or I'll be calling in the police.

Night after night after night my good lady and I lie awake forcibly listening to that stereo of yours and if it's not the stereo it's the TV and if it's not the TV it's the lot of you charging about knocking things over and making a general hullabaloo.

This is your final warning.

It's the police next time. Plus the council, who are very hot on noise nuisance, I gather.

At least this letter gets the subject of complaint into the first paragraph.

But if the nearest to a formal rebuke has previously been a lot of knuckle-bruising on the bedroom wall, the threats and general tone are premature.

If the neighbours are that noisy, they probably have

not even heard the drumming on the wall. They may be absolute pigs, but it is better to start with the assumption, however unlikely, that they have no idea what a nuisance they have been creating.

The threats, the police and the Noise Abatement Man can come later, if necessary.

TRY THIS INSTEAD

> My wife and I are regularly kept awake by loud sounds from your house in the early hours. Last night, for example, pop music was still playing loudly at three a.m.

> You may not realise how easily the sound from stereo, TV and even loud conversation can go through the party wall.

> We would be grateful if you would reduce the amount of late-night disturbance.

Life and people being what they are, you will no doubt need to turn to officialdom in the end. But your opening shot will read most reasonably in court.

To a holiday firm that let you down

> My wife and I have just returned from a quite expensive holiday booked through your firm and I have to state that it was utterly disappointing.

> Call yourself a tour operator? Don't make me laugh. The things you promised in that brochure of yours, it turned out to be nothing like, from the state of the pool to the food, etcetera.

> We are hereby demanding a refund of at least £1,000 on it.

Supposing you are lucky enough to have booked with
76

one of the dwindling number of tour firms staying in business, you will need to be much more explicit about what was wrong with the holiday you paid for.

It may also be a mistake to offer an *at least* settlement figure, because that immediately becomes, to the holiday firm, *at most* – at best.

The first paragraph is reasonably direct, though *I have to state* is a waste of space (see *Witter Words*, p. 38). But then the letter becomes vague as well as sneery. You have to set out your complaints, one by one, against the promises of the brochure.

> The hotel pool was unusable: there were still many traces of the recent rainstorm of bats' blood and giant frogs, during which the cover was apparently left off.

> Meal service, described in the brochure as 'super de luxe attention par excellence', was inexcusably slow. My wife's *turbot à la Japon* was eventually brought to us in the bar, shortly after we had ordered teatime cocktails.

> It also smelt unpleasant and we put it straight into the dustbin for fear of food poisoning. This obviously does not support the brochure's claim that food at our hotel was the 'creme de la creme of the Costas'.

> The hotel itself looks out on to a derelict filling station, tyre dump, sewage farm and train shed, according to where you stand. We could not see the sea, golden sands, waving palm trees or quaint whitewashed villas not only described but also pictured in the brochure.

> My wife was especially disturbed by one room-service waiter, who each morning barged into our room on some pretext or other, always managing to catch her, a mature lady, half-dressed or completely naked.

This unfortunate timing was explained when we discovered a peephole in the door. I tackled the waiter about it and he hit me in the mouth, knocking out two teeth.

I complained about all this to the reception clerk, who merely shrugged and said: 'A lady so old and fat should be so lucky, and you still got plenty teeth.'

Finally, our baggage was apparently stolen from a 'secure storage space' before it even left the hotel on our journey home.

Please let me know, within seven days, your proposals for compensation over this entirely unsatisfactory holiday.

To an interfering Granny

Bill and I are both fed up to the teeth with the way you keep trying to force us into sending our kids – *our* kids, not yours – to a private school when that is completely against our principles.

Opening a fund for the fees without asking us first was bad enough.

Constantly telling the kids how lovely it was going to be was even worse.

Now you have had the audacity to put their names down for, in one case, Eton, and in the other case, Roedean. Yuk!

This nonsense has got to stop. Until we have your solemn written promise to leave the education of our children to us, their parents, you will not see either of them again.

And don't bother contacting your precious son, either, because he agrees with me!

Well, that certainly told Granny, didn't it? You could scarcely be accused of lack of clarity, conciseness and directness. Or that valuable attribute, low cunning.

Every family, of course, has its own grievances, loathings, jealousies and obstinacies. Only the details vary. So it may just be possible to tiptoe into this particular affray and suggest how, although the battle has clearly been going on for years, the softer approach might – just *might* – achieve the desired end, which is to Stop Granny Interfering So Much.

TRY THIS WAY

> You already know how Bill and I feel about private schools, and although your generosity would otherwise have been appreciated, we do not think it is fair of you to go over our heads as you have been doing.

> Obviously, wherever you have put our children's names down, there is no chance of their going to those schools. So the result is just confusing to them, a waste of staff time and money for the school – and a waste of our own time and money making sure the school is not misled about our intentions.

> We know you worry about your grandchildren's future, and we share your worry. We just have different ways of trying to cope with it.

> We don't want the children to become victims of a battle between you and us. But we have to answer for their welfare in every way.

> Could you think about dropping the private-school idea? There is so much else you could do for them – such as music and riding lessons.

It might lack the fun of all-out warfare. But there is a chance that Granny might calm down.

Spare the Comma, Spoil the Sentence

Writers often worry about commas and other punctuation. What to use, when to use it.

This is not a guide to grammar (see *Good Grammar in One Hour*, Mandarin, £2.99). But it is an attempt to help you write clearly as well as concisely. And misused, misplaced punctuation can cause confusion.

You may have been taught never to put a comma before *and*. Discard the advice. Advancing through the language jungle, treat your comma as an ever-ready hip-flask, available for any emergency. If your sentence looks like flagging without one, administer a strong comma, at once.

Too many commas, spattered pedantically about your page, can just get in the way. But if you are too miserly with them, the reader may be left to puzzle out where the sentence is supposed to be going. Or, just as likely, he or she will give up and read something else.

Watch where you put them

An ill-placed comma can completely alter the sense of what you write.

> Women who are bad drivers present a danger to the public.

No doubt as true of women as of men. But see how peril on the road can spread, if the writer gets comma-happy:

> Women, who are bad drivers, present a danger to the public.

Confusion can also be caused when your sentence needs a single comma, but you use more:

RIGHT: The driver having been charged, the police phoned his wife.
WRONG: The driver, having been charged, the police phoned his wife.

That comma after *driver* leads the reader to believe that you are about to reveal what the driver did next, not what someone else – in this example, the police – did next. You have just given the reader an unnecessary jolt. Too much of that, and you are likely to lose your reader altogether.

A comma-free solution, of course, would be:

After the driver was charged the police phoned his wife.

There is an argument for a comma after charged, but you can do without it. Suit yourself, it's a free comma!

You don't always have to use them

Many sentences, even quite long ones, are instantly understandable without a comma in sight. Others are not.

One that is:

I do not suggest there is ever likely to be another politician whose standing in the eyes of the public comes anywhere near to equalling that of the late Sir Winston Churchill in the earliest stage of the Second World War.

One that is not:

There were of course going to be exceptions to the rule as with any field of human activity though this was no reason he pointed out why the courts should slacken in their response to the problems of crime in general.

This stumbler needs four commas to pick it up off the pavement.

There were of course going to be exceptions to the rule, as with any field of human activity, though this was no reason, he pointed out, why the courts should slacken in their response to the problems of crime in general.

Beware of overdosing

You could shovel in even more commas:

There were, of course, going to be exceptions to the rule, as with any field of human activity, though this was no reason, he pointed out, why the courts should slacken, in their response to the problems of crime, in general.

But that, as the jargon goes, might be three or four commas too far.

Every little comma has a meaning of its own

The comma may be a mere speck of ink on the paper, but, properly used, it can add nuance and intrigue, as well as clarity, to a statement.

I walked into the room and found the gasman there.

So what? He's only looking for the meter. But now add a comma.

I walked into the room, and found the gasman there.

82

Hello, hello, hello – what's going on here? Your comma has introduced a tiny hesitancy into the sentence. A suggestion that something is not quite right, or ordinary, about the gasman's presence.

If you really want to point the finger, try a loaded full stop instead.

> I walked into the room. And found the gasman there.

A comma is not a full stop

One firm DON'T is: DON'T use a comma instead of a full stop:

> He said he was just going to the pub, he never returned.

There are two separate statements. The comma leads your reader to expect another one, to complete the sentence:

> He said he was just going to the pub, he never returned and we have not seen him again to this day.

If you want your two statements in a single sentence, insert *but* before *he never*. Then you can keep your comma or take it out, as you please. Otherwise, take out the comma and put in a full stop.

> He said he was just going to the pub. He never returned.

Make a dash for it

The dash is another useful piece of equipment in your journey through the jungle.

A single dash serves to add emphasis to a phrase or word:

> He opened the envelope, which was not properly sealed and found – a cheque.

The single dash can also be used to attach a comment to a sentence:

> He opened the envelope, which was not properly sealed, and found a cheque – at last.

A pair of dashes is useful to fence off a thought that is an aside:

> He opened the envelope – it was not properly sealed – and found a cheque.

Try not to get too fond of dashes. They can turn your writing into a scatty, breathless mess:

> He went to the front door – the postman had just been – and found an envelope – not properly sealed – in which was a cheque.

Ration yourself to no more than one or two every fourth or fifth paragraph.

Case for the colon . . .

The colon (:) is often used instead of a full stop. The liveliest explanation of what a colon is for comes in *Fowler's Modern English Usage* (Oxford University Press): 'delivering the goods that have been invoiced in the preceding words'.

> It was not so much the mystery of the vanished gas meter: that, it turned out, was only the beginning.

Nobody would really quarrel with a full stop there, but the colon has us on our toes, waiting for the follow-up.

. . . and the semi-colon

It is possible to get through life without feeling the need of a single semi-colon. But the semi-colon is a useful instrument to have in your writer's toolkit.

You may have two statements which could be given as separate sentences, but which are so closely linked that a full stop seems too much of an interruption in the flow of thought. Using a full stop:

> He is doing well, so far. I just wish he had improved much earlier.

Using a semi-colon:

> He is doing well, so far; I just wish he had improved much earlier.

A semi-colon is useful also when you have a sentence containing several commas, and in which you need a stronger break, at some point. Without the semi-colon:

> She thought back to the hurtful things he had said to her, about her face, her figure, her hair, her clothes, jibes for which he would never be able to make amends.

There is a slightly bewildering effect, when the lady's plaintive catalogue ends on a mere comma.

Replace the last comma with a semi-colon:

> She thought back to the hurtful things he had said to her, about her face, her figure, her hair, her clothes; jibes for which he would never be able to make amends.

Measure the Blinding Fog

The Fog Index, to measure the readability of a piece of writing, was invented by an American anti-jargon pro-clarity crusader named Robert Gunning.

A Fog Index of 13 or over is a warning that the writer may have made the going unnecessarily heavy for the reader. However, this is *not* a template to work with when you write – and it is fallible. Treat the Fog Index as a semi-serious guide to the clarity of what you have written.

This is how it works:

Choose a section of the written work, at least 100 words long. Count the number of words. Divide the total by the number of sentences. That will give you the average sentence length. If a long sentence contains two or more complete thoughts, separated by a comma, colon or semi-colon, treat each thought as a sentence, for the purpose of judging clarity.

Now go through the same passage, counting the words of three or more syllables. Ignore proper names and words which become three-syllable only because *-ed*, *-s* or *-es* has been added to the basic word – for example, *invent-ed*, *transpose-s*. Also ignore words formed by combining short, simple words: *caretaker*, *maneater*.

Get out the calculator and find the *percentage* of multi-syllable words (*Divide* multi-syllable total by word total, *multiply* result by 100).

Add your average-sentence-length figure to your multi-syllable-percentage figure. *Multiply* the total by 0.4.

The result is the FOG INDEX for that piece of writing.

Let us try this Fog Index test on some examples of published work.

A leading article in the *Sun* newspaper:

> A fortnight today Britain's future in Europe will be decided. /
>
> Not by the voters of Britain, / but by the voters of France. /
>
> Our Government has made it clear that if the French say 'Non' in their referendum, the Maastricht Treaty is dead. /
>
> If they say 'Oui', we can all go happily forward / with no regard to how the British people may feel. /
>
> This is unacceptable. /
>
> Our people have never had the chance to vote on European unity. /
>
> Maastricht was not an Election issue / so it is quite arguable that Britain should have a referendum. /
>
> Mr Major believes that this kind of poll is 'undemocratic'. /
>
> Surely it can't be wrong if the ordinary man and woman – as well as MPs – have their say. /

Total words: 122. Over two syllables: 11. Percentage: 9.
Total sentences: 12. Average sentence length: 10.

Add 10 and 9 = 19. Multiply by 0.4.

FOG INDEX: **7.6**   Sparklingly clear.

From the *Sunday Telegraph* editorial on the same topic:

> The spectacle of the French being allowed their say, / while the British people are silenced, / grows daily more intolerable. / We seldom have anything to learn about democracy from the land of Robespierre and Bonaparte, / but we do now. / On September 20 French voters will have the chance to give their verdict on the Maastricht Treaty, / and

our own Government has said it will be bound by their decision. /

The leaders of both main parties have conspired to supress debate about Europe, / which they know would expose deep divisions among their followers. / They prevented Europe from becoming an issue in our general election / by the simple expedient of agreeing with each other. / The voter wishing to register his or her opposition to Maastricht was given no serious party for which to vote. /

Our politicians have thereby spared themselves the disagreeable task of justifying their European policy to the public. /

Total words: 149. Over two syllables: 16. Percentage: 10. Total sentences: 13. Average length: 11.5.

Add 11.5 and 10 = 21.5. Multiply by 0.4.

FOG INDEX: **8.6** Despite the more elaborate construction, hardly less clear than the tabloid *Sun*.

From an editorial in the *Independent* newspaper:

More worldly ministerial advisers than the bishop might have put the issue with great cynicism yesterday: / There is little to be gained by further flogging a dead horse. / If the TUC is not dead, it is possibly in terminal decline / after 13 years of maltreatment by Conservative administrations. / Moreover, the emergence of a handful of super-unions, well able to handle their own affairs and to offer their members the material benefits associated with service unionism, / makes it hard to see the purpose of a large and costly central union bureaucracy. /

Some of the more optimistic delegates gathered at Blackpool are taking consolation from the fact that the Secretary of State for Employment, Gillian

Shephard, is demonstrably bored with the plans for further union reforms inherited from her predecessor, Michael Howard, who delighted in reviving the union bogey. / She will push ahead with his proposals to introduce greater freedom for workers to join the union of their choice / and to render more difficult the system of 'check off' / (under which employers deduct union dues from workers' pay packets), / then turn her mind to questions of industrial training and job creation. /

Total words: 191. Over two syllables: 27. Percentage: 14. Total sentences: 11. Average length: 17.

Add 17 and 14 = 31. Multiply by 0.4.

FOG INDEX: **12.4**   Dangerously close to the edge of the fog.

From *The Second World War: Triumph and Tragedy*, by Winston Churchill, regarded as a master of English prose:

The final destruction of the German Army has been related; it remains to describe the end of Hitler's other fighting forces. / During the previous autumn the German Air Force, / by a remarkable feat of organisation, / but at the cost of its long-range bomber output, / had greatly increased the number of its fighter aircraft. / Our strategic bombing had thrown it on to the defensive / and 70 per cent of its fighters had to be used for home defence. / Although greater in numbers their effectiveness was less, largely owing to fuel shortage caused by our attacks on oil installations, / which it became their principal duty to prevent. / German high-performance jet fighters perturbed us for a time, / but special raids on their centres of production and their airfields averted the threat. / Throughout January and February our bombers continued to attack, / and we made a heavy raid in the latter month on Dresden, then a centre of communications of Germany's Eastern Front. / The enemy air was fading. / As our troops advanced the airfields of the Luftwaffe were more and more squeezed into a diminishing area, / and provided excellent targets. /

Total words: 186. Over two syllables: 13. Percentage: 6.98.
Total sentences: 17. Average length: 11.

Add 11 and 6.98 = 17.98. Multiply by 0.4.

FOG INDEX: 7.2   Churchill remains an example to us all.

From *The Way through the Woods*, by Colin Dexter:

As he had just considered the photographs, it was the man himself, pictured in two of them, who had monopolized his interest: / a small- to medium-sized man, in his late twenties perhaps, with longish fair hair; / a man wearing a white T-shirt and faded-blue denims, / with a sunburnt complexion and the suggestion of a day's growth of stubble around his jowls. / But the detail was not of sufficient definition or fidelity for him to be wholly sure, / as if the cameraman himself –/ or almost certainly the camerawoman –/ had scarcely the experience needed to cope with the problems of the bright sunlight that so obviously pervaded the garden in which the snaps had been taken./

Total words: 117. Over two syllables: 12. Percentage: 10.25.
Total sentences: 8. Average length: 14.6.

Add 14.6 and 10.25 = 24.85. Multiply by 0.4.

FOG INDEX: **9.9**   Well clear of the mist.

**Letter from Queen Victoria to Sir Robert Peel,
7 September 1841:**

> The Queen wishes that Sir Robert Peel would men-
> tion to Lord De la Warr / that he should be very
> particular in always naming to the Queen any
> appointment he wishes to make in his department, /
> and always to take her pleasure upon an appoint-
> ment before he settles on them; / this is a point
> upon which the Queen has always laid great stress. /
> This applies in great measure to the appointment of
> Physicians and Chaplains, / which used to be very
> badly managed formerly, / and who were appointed
> in a very careless manner; / but since the Queen's
> accession the Physicians and Chaplains have been
> appointed only for merit and abilities, by the Queen
> herself, / which the Queen is certain Sir Robert Peel
> will at once see is a far better way, / and one which
> must be of use in every way.

Total words: 143. Over two syllables: 13. Percentage: 9.
Total sentences: 10. Average length: 12.

Add 12 and 9 = 21. Multiply by 0.4.

FOG INDEX: **8.4**   Well done, Your Late Majesty!

**From *A Good Enough Parent: the guide to bringing
up your child* by Bruno Bettelheim (Thames and
Hudson):**

Psychoanalytic doctrine is deeply committed to the
conviction that how these inherited characteristics
will be shaped depends on a person's life experi-

ences. / Thus it subscribes to a historical view, / according to which later events are to a considerable degree conditioned by what has happened before; / therefore, the earliest history of the individual is of greatest importance in respect to what he will be like in his later life, / not only because it is the basis for all that follows but also because early history largely determines how later life will be experienced. / While genetic and evolutionary history creates an individual's potentialities, / his early personal history more than anything that follows accounts for the forms these potentialities will take in the actuality of his life. /

Total words: 125. Over two syllables: 20. Percentage: 16.
Total sentences: 7. Average length: 17.8.

Add 17.8 and 16 = 33.8. Multiply by 0.4.

FOG INDEX: **13.5** Not the kind of writing to struggle with if you're looking for urgent help to fend off an enraged infant.

Yet the Bettelheim is lucid, compared with this example from our Officialese section (p. 10):

A person shall be treated as suffering from physical disablement such that he is either unable to walk or virtually unable to do so if he is not unable or virtually unable to walk with a prosthesis or an artificial aid which he habitually wears or uses or if he would not be unable or virtually unable to walk if he habitually wore or used a prosthesis or an artificial aid which is suitable in his case. /

Total words: 78. Over two syllables: 19. Percentage: 24.
Total sentences: 1 (The sheer overall obscurity prevents

our splitting this piece into sub-sentences.) Average sentence length: 78.

Add 78 and 24 = 102. Multiply by 0.4.

FOG INDEX: an impenetrable **40.8**   Someone was unable, or virtually unable, to write English – prosthesis or no prosthesis.

Testing the experts' expert – *Fowler's Modern English Usage*:

> The use of semi-colons to separate parallel expressions that would normally be separated by commas is not in itself illegitimate, / but it must not be done when the expressions so separated form a group that is itself separated by nothing more than a comma, if that, from another part of the sentence. / To do this is to make the less include the greater, / which is absurd . . . /
>
> . . . As long as the Prayer-Book version of the Psalms continues to be read, the colon is not likely to pass quite out of use as a stop, / chiefly as one preferred to the semi-colon by individuals, or in impressive contexts, or in gnomic contrasts (Man proposes: God disposes); / but the time when it was second member of the hierarchy, full stop, colon, semi-colon, comma, is past.

Total words: 133. Over two syllables: 12. Percentage: 9. Total sentences: 6. Average length: 22.

Add 9 and 22 = 31. Multiply by 0.4.

FOG INDEX: **12.4**   Just the right side of the fog bank, according to Robert Gunning's test.

As we said, the Fog Index is fallible. You would expect

the extract to get the all-clear: after all, it was written
by that master of correct language, H.W. Fowler,
author of *Modern English Usage*. The extract was in
fact taken from a revised edition of the book produced
by that apostle of plain English, Sir Ernest Gowers.
And it does get the all-clear, just.

But there is another test by which that excerpt would
get a much worse score for unreadability. It's the
Commonsense Test.

Wonders of the Word Processor

If you do a lot of writing, you probably already own a computer word processor. For those still holding back from the 'new' technology, here are a few processed words on its advantages – and drawbacks.

A word processor will do more tricks than a mere glorified typewriter. But a glorified typewriter is what most writers want.

Its biggest single advantage is that it lets you play around with the words on screen until you have got them right. Whole blocks of text, or a single word, can be moved up and down the page, or deleted, without so much as the rustle of a sheet of A4.

The writer yearning for perfection might think hard before deciding to mess up a much-revised page with correcting fluid, or use scissors and paste and then type the whole thing again.

With a word processor, you leave the satisfactory bits alone and fiddle only with the unsatisfactory bits. Then, when all is ready, you print your document.

How does it work?

The cheaper types of word processor need to be fed with instructions from a removable disc, each time you switch on. Dearer models have a built-in 'hard disc' which also has to be fed, but only once.

There is a wide range of word-processing languages, some easier to use than others. Some of the most popular are Wordperfect and Wordstar. Some work by a 'menu' list of instructions for you to choose from; others wait for you to enter a simple code from the keyboard.

Your writings are recorded on either a removable disc or the hard disc. The hard version can hold a stupendous amount of work. Even the removable kind can contain an entire book.

More attractive display becomes possible: you should be able to use italics, bold face, underscore and a variety of small, large or condensed type.

The work comes out on a printer attached to the computer: the printer may not be able to handle all the fancy touches which the computer offers, but there should be enough to help you smarten up your printed page.

If possible, get a friend who is already using a computer to help you through the earliest phase of getting to know yours. The manual supplied may not be a model of clarity, and many a beginner has come near to blows with his machine before it agreed to understand his wishes.

Read the words on the screen with extra care until you get used to your new machine: it is surprisingly easy to miss a mistake which might have glared at you from a printed page. And because adjustments are so easy, you may be tempted to waste a lot of paper, making your document ever more beautiful.